I0884170

DISCOVERING AMERICA
★ An Exceptional Nation ★

Politics and Power in the United States

Kristin Thiel

Cavendish Square
New York

Published in 2019 by Cavendish Square Publishing, LLC
243 5th Avenue, Suite 136, New York, NY 10016

First Edition

Cataloging-in-Publication Data

Names: Thiel, Kristin.
Title: Politics and power in the United States / Kristin Thiel.
Description: New York : Cavendish Square, 2019. |
Series: Discovering America | Includes glossary and index.
Identifiers: ISBN 9781502643506 (pbk.) | ISBN 9781502642615 (library bound) |
ISBN 9781502643513 (ebook)
Subjects: LCSH: United States--Politics and government--Juvenile literature.
Classification: LCC JK40.T47 2019 | DDC 320.473--dc23

Editorial Director: David McNamara
Editor: Caitlyn Miller
Copy Editor: Rebecca Rohan
Associate Art Director: Alan Sliwinski
Designer: Joe Parenteau
Production Coordinator: Karol Szymczuk
Photo Research: J8 Media

The photographs in this book are used by permission and through the courtesy of: Cover Orhan Cam/Shutterstock.com; p. 4 Victorian Traditions/Shutterstock.com; p. 7 Science History Images/Alamy Stock Photo; p. 14, 34, 45, 81 MPI/Getty Images; p. 16 Ullstein Bild/Getty Images; p. 25 Howard Chandler Christy/Wikimedia Commons/File:Scene at the Signing of the Constitution of the United States.jpg/Public Domain; p. 26 (and used throughout) Tgavrano/Shutterstock.com; p. 27 Archive Photos/Getty Images; p. 31, 90 Hulton Archive/Getty Images; p. 32 Kean Collection/Getty Images; p. 36, 53 Stock Montage/Getty Images; p. 42, 50 North Wind Picture Archives; p. 52 Library of Congress/Getty Images; p. 58, 72, 85 Bettmann/Corbis; p. 64 Chicago History Museum/Getty Images; p. 67 Library of Congress; p. 79 Michal812/Shutterstock.com; p. 87 Lee Lockwood/The LIFE Images Collection/Getty Images; p. 94 Universal History Archive/Getty Images; p. 96 Drew Angerer/Getty Images.

Printed in the United States of America

CONTENTS

Founding Fathers Benjamin Franklin (*left*), John Adams (*center*), and Thomas Jefferson (*right*) consider a draft of the Declaration of Independence.

Chapter One

Governing a New Nation: 1491 to 1800

The founders of the United States designed the country's system of power and governance to be accessible to everyday citizens, not just to its elected and appointed leaders. Each branch of government is accountable to the people, and each wields checks and balances over the other branches. No one segment of government is entrusted with complete power. This distribution of power has had a major effect on how the country has evolved over time, and the emphasis on the power of the people begins with the country's early influences.

Native American Influence

The United States can trace the inspiration for its government back to the ancient Greeks, but some of its greatest ideas may have come more directly from within the country's own borders. In 1988, the US government officially resolved that the Founding Fathers, particularly George Washington and Benjamin Franklin, developed some of their ideas about government out of their admiration of the Iroquois government. Concurrent Resolution 331 went on to say that "the confederation of the original Thirteen Colonies into one republic was influenced by the political system developed by the Iroquois Confederacy as were many of the democratic principles which were incorporated into the Constitution itself." In other words, the writers of the US Constitution modeled that document on the work of the Iroquois people. There is evidence to support other Native groups also inspiring the Founding Fathers.

The Original American Union

In the late 1500s, the Iroquois Confederacy, or Iroquois League, formed in what is now upstate New York. This group of Native peoples became one of the most powerful precolonial groups in the United States. The confederacy was also known as Five Nations, referring to the Haudenosaunee, or Iroquois, nations of Mohawk,

A depiction of the Iroquois Confederacy dating from 1724.

Seneca, Onondaga, Oneida, and Cayuga. It was later known as Six Nations, when the Tuscarora people joined. These groups described themselves as "the people of the longhouse," meaning they shared a type of architecture: long, one-story houses made of saplings.

A man named Dekanawidah started the Iroquois's unification process. He also is the narrator of the Great Law of Peace, the constitution that the unified tribes followed. This document begins by stating that a Tree of Great Peace, also called the Tree of the Great Long Leaves, has been planted. Its roots of peace and strength spread in the four cardinal directions, north, east, south, and west. An eagle sits on the highest branches, keeping watch for approaching danger. This tree's power is available to everyone: "If any man or any nation … shall obey the laws of the Great Peace … they may trace the Roots to the Tree and if their minds are clean and they are obedient and promise to obey the wishes of the Confederate Council, they shall be welcomed to take shelter beneath the Tree of the Long Leaves."

Each of the six tribes had one vote in the confederacy's council; all decisions had to be unanimous to pass. Leaders were voted into office. When they negotiated with the colonies, both sides followed the Iroquois Confederacy's negotiation process and rituals.

Native-Colonist Alliances and the End of a Nation

Around the turn of the seventeenth century, the confederacy of what was then five nations faced danger from both white colonists and their Huron and Mohican neighbors. As the Iroquois traded more frequently with colonists, exchanging beaver pelts for guns, the Iroquois attacked their Native neighbors more frequently as well. They needed access to more land so they could get animals for their trade, and eventually, the confederacy stretched from the St. Lawrence River south into Pennsylvania and west into Illinois. The Iroquois also fought against the French colonists, who were allies of the Iroquois's enemies, the Algonquin and the Huron tribes. This aligned the Iroquois with the British, who were enemies of the French.

During the American Revolution, the Iroquois Confederacy was divided over which side to support. The Oneida and the Tuscarora sided with the colonist Patriots, while the other four Iroquois groups fought for the British Loyalists. Because most members aligned with what would be the losing side of the revolution, the confederacy soon ended. The Second Treaty of Fort Stanwix in 1784 made this dissolution official.

Experts think the United States may have been influenced by the Iroquois for several reasons. First, the leaders of the colonists and the Iroquois were familiar with each other. In 1744, Canassatego, a chief of the Onondaga tribe, spoke to colonial representatives in Lancaster, Pennsylvania. He suggested the colonists follow the Iroquois Confederacy's model, saying, "We are a powerful Confederacy; and, by your observing the same Methods our wise Forefathers have taken, you will acquire fresh Strength and Power."

Second, the Iroquois Confederacy and United States' systems of government have clear similarities that were recorded in writing. In 1754, colonial representatives met at the Albany Congress to discuss working together for the first time. Some of the ideas presented there mirrored those of the Iroquois. Benjamin Franklin, who had published a transcript of Canassatego's speech, presented some of Canassatego's ideas in his Albany Plan. Later, during the 1780s debates about the Constitution, the Founding Fathers referenced the confederacy's practices. In his 1787 book *Defence* [sic] *of the Constitutions of Government of the United States*, John Adams, who would become the second US president, said it would be wise to study the Iroquois ways. Furthermore, both governments operated on local levels and centralized levels—in other words, government at the level of both the tribes/states and the Iroquois Confederacy/US federal government.

(There are historians, however, who do not think the Iroquois Confederacy had particular influence on the formation of the US government. They cite differences between the two groups, like the role heredity played in how the Iroquois chose leaders and how little population mattered when they selected representation.)

The Original American Nomination Process

Caucuses are an American invention, originating with the Algonquin tribe. Today, states have either primaries or caucuses—though a couple have both. Instead of privately voting on a ballot during a primary, in a caucus system, neighbors meet in person to discuss candidates.

The word "caucus" comes from the Algonquin word "caw-cawaasough," meaning "one who advises, a counselor." Colonists admired how the Algonquins expressed their opinions one at a time without interruption during debate. This was quite different from the British system in which members of Parliament were expected to outshout each other to win a debate.

The term "caucus clubs" appeared in John Adams's journals as early as 1763. By 1809, political candidates were chosen in closed-door caucuses. By 1830, caucuses were open to the public. They were the main way states chose candidates through 1972.

Early Colonial Governments

Today, we think of the original European colonists as part of one unit: the thirteen colonies. In actuality, each colony formed in its own time, for its own reasons, and with its own unique group of people.

For example, the Virginia Company of London founded Virginia. The colony was owned by shareholders, just as individuals own stock in corporations. The ships that left England for Virginia in 1606 were filled with men and boys only. Their one mission was to work and make a profit for the company.

The middle colony of New York started as New Netherland because the Dutch owned it. People from the Netherlands, as well as Belgian Flemings and Walloons, French Huguenots, Scandinavians, and Germans, lived there. In 1664, the English moved in and renamed the colony after York, England.

Pennsylvania, also a middle colony, was founded by a wealthy individual, William Penn. Penn's Woods, which is what the name Pennsylvania means, was a haven for Quakers. They also preached religious tolerance for followers of other religions.

Before the colonies were ready to unify as one country and explore ideas of centralized government, they each set up their own political system.

The Mayflower Compact

The 102 passengers of the *Mayflower* did not have an easy arrival in the colonies in 1620. They were forty-one Pilgrims, people seeking freedom from the Church of England, and sixty-one "strangers," as the Pilgrims called them. They were strangers to each other too—they were an unrelated collection of workers, indentured servants, and young orphans. Therefore, they were not a unified group. Then they missed their intended landing spot: the passengers had signed a contract with the Virginia Company to land in Virginia, but they ended up landing in Massachusetts. Many of the people aboard the *Mayflower* said that meant their agreement with Virginia no longer existed. In fact, they believed that meant they did not have to follow any rules.

The *Mayflower* passengers realized they had better establish guidelines before chaos ensued. As a result, they wrote what is called the Mayflower Compact. This was the first set of laws in the American colonies that a group wrote to govern itself. Everyone who signed the document pledged to remain loyal to the British government, live as Christians, and work together to create one society, including enacting laws. Historians credit the Mayflower Compact with helping keep the Plymouth Colony, as the passengers called their new home, going through the first deadly winter. More than half of the colonists died that winter; if the group had not been unified beforehand, the survivors may have lost hope. Instead, the survivors worked together to stay alive. The Mayflower Compact, intended to help the colonists temporarily, lasted until 1691, when the Plymouth colonists became Massachusetts colonists.

Virginia's House of Burgesses

The House of Burgesses was the first governing body with democratically elected officials in the American colonies. Its first meeting was in Jamestown, Virginia, in July 1619. Each county in the colony was allowed to elect and send to the house two burgesses, or representatives. Larger towns could request to be allowed to send their own delegate. As one of the first universities in the colonies, the College of William and Mary even sent a burgess. When the House of Burgesses started, it had twenty-two members. They made laws and responded to settlement requests for supplies.

Founding Fathers George Washington, Thomas Jefferson, Richard Henry Lee, and Patrick Henry all

The first assembly of the House of Burgesses met in 1619.

served in the House of Burgesses. Nathaniel Bacon was also a burgess. From 1676 to 1677, Bacon led a rebellion against Virginia's Native American allies and, by extension, the colony's governor. A small-scale civil war broke out between Bacon's followers and the governor's. Bacon's army even burned the colony's capital. After Bacon's Rebellion, British King Charles II began limiting the activities of legislatures like the House of Burgesses.

By the beginning of the 1700s, the governing body had much less power than before but was still important. At first, the burgesses helped wealthy tobacco plantation owners. Starting in 1764, they sided with the colonists as a whole. The British Parliament had begun taxing the colonies after the French and Indian War. The burgesses protested so much against the Stamp Act in 1765 that they were almost charged with treason. After the burgesses supported the Boston Tea Party, the British dissolved the group. However, the burgesses regrouped on their own. Their work led to the First Continental Congress, the colonies' combined protest against taxation without representation.

The Enlightenment and the Great Awakening

External government structures and legal documents were not the only influences on the colonies. The Enlightenment and the Great Awakening were two philosophical movements that directly inspired the American Revolution.

The Enlightenment

The Enlightenment affected European society from 1685 to 1815. Because of Europe's position as a world power, the Age of Reason, as it was also called, spread to other parts of the world, including the American colonies. Isaac Newton, who determined how gravity worked, helped usher in the Enlightenment. His book on the laws of motion and gravity, *Philosophiae Naturalis Principia Mathematica* (*Mathematical Principles of Natural Philosophy*), was published in 1687.

Enlightenment thinkers in every field from politics to science suggested that logic and rationality could change humanity for the better and make amends for past beliefs.

For example, the famous astronomer Galileo earned some acceptance during the Enlightenment, which happened decades after his death. Galileo's observations of the solar system contradicted the teachings of the Catholic Church. The Church brought him to trial, and he died under house arrest. Enlightenment leaders like Voltaire argued that Galileo's name should be cleared. The Catholic Church ultimately removed one of his books from its banned books list in 1744.

During the Enlightenment, John Locke, who studied philosophy and political theory, greatly influenced the American Founding Fathers from his home in England. His "Two Treatises of Government," which was published in 1690, contradicted traditional belief that God had given ultimate power to kings and queens. Instead, Locke argued, the people of a country held the true power—they were the ones who formed their government. Thomas Jefferson included Locke's idea that people could remove their leaders from power in the Declaration of Independence in 1776.

English philosopher John Locke influenced the views of the US Founding Fathers.

In Locke's three "Letters Concerning Toleration," published over the years of 1689 to 1692, Locke supported religious freedom (to a degree). He also said that governments had no right to show favor to one religion over another—in other words, he suggested the separation of church and state.

The Enlightenment became a powerful force in the colonies. In 1732, King George II allowed James Oglethorpe, a social reformer and member of Parliament, to start the colony of Georgia. Oglethorpe created the colony with Enlightenment ideals. He wanted it to be a place where people with little money could start over. He gave each male immigrant land and supplies. The Oglethorpe Plan focused on farming as the primary industry and equality as the primary philosophy. He even banned slavery. (Whites who moved to Georgia from colonies that allowed slavery ignored the ban, and by the 1850s, slavery was a major part of Georgia's society.)

Perhaps the most prominent Enlightenment thinker in the colonies, however, was Benjamin Franklin. His American Philosophical Society, founded in 1743, had the goal of improving colonists' lives by encouraging people to think critically. He was a deist, meaning he believed in God and reason outside of religion. His study of electricity demonstrated the practical applications of the Enlightenment: not only did he make the connection between metal and lightning but he suggested that metal poles, called lightning rods, could attract the bolts of electricity and redirect them from wooden buildings, which could catch on fire.

The Great Awakening

The Great Awakening influenced the American colonies during the 1730s and 1740s. It was, to a degree, a reaction to the Enlightenment. During a time of such focus on secular reason, some people wished for a religious balance. Yet there was no unifying religious movement in the colonies—colonists were Quakers, Anglicans, Lutherans, Baptists, Presbyterians, and members of the Dutch Reformed Church. The Great Awakening filled that gap.

Jonathan Edwards, an Anglican minister, was considered a founder of the Great Awakening. He preached the movement's main points: everyone was born a sinner, and if you did not receive forgiveness from God, you went to hell when you died. Though he usually preached in his hometown of Northampton, Massachusetts, his sermons were shared throughout the colonies.

The message of the Great Awakening spread so well in part because most ministers traveled. In one year, a British minister named George Whitefield preached to the colonists more than 350 times. Some of his audiences numbered more than a thousand people. He crisscrossed the colonies, logging thousands of miles that year.

Most ministers also believed church was for everyone, no matter race or class. They urged people to form a personal connection with God. Eternal life was at stake, so they should not allow ministers to be the middlemen between them and God.

Ultimately, the Great Awakening helped form America's religious foundation. It also encouraged colonists toward the American Revolution. In the 1600s and 1700s, colonists lived in relatively unconnected villages. There were few roads and no national mail system. Most people didn't get newspapers. They got their information from Bibles and sermons: the average New England colonist heard fifteen thousand hours of preaching. They were taught that God saw them as free people. They debated issues of authority, both spiritual and legal, in church. Humans were not above God, the ministers taught, so governments—like the British monarchy and Parliament—should not have the power they did over the colonists. The Bible was full of stories of oppressed people fighting for the freedom God said they should have. When the colonists turned against the British, they did so for lots of reasons, both rational and religious.

The United States Makes Its First International Alliance

The summer of 1776 was an uncomfortable one in Philadelphia. The weather was hot, and the political situation was stickier: the colonists had been fighting the British for more than a year.

American colonists' dislike of their British rulers had been growing since 1764. That was the year the British

Parliament passed the Stamp Act. The colonists disagreed with being taxed without having representation in the British government. In other words, they were forced to carry a heavy financial weight, but they were not allowed to have any power.

The colonists did not jump immediately to war. They tried to protest Britain's laws in meaningful but more contained ways. In 1771, two thousand North Carolina farmers led a huge armed rebellion against their British governor's tax plan. The government's militia easily defeated the farmers in the Battle of Alamance and demanded the colonists publicly swear allegiance to England. When Massachusetts colonists protested the Tea Act of 1773 with the Boston Tea Party, Britain punished them with more restrictive laws.

The colonists did not seem able to win, and compromise between the two sides did not seem possible. Early in the morning on April 19, 1775, the colonies' war for independence began. The first gunshot of the war is often called the "shot heard 'round the world." It was an impressive colonial uprising, lasting until the signing of the Treaty of Paris in 1783. The independent nation of the United States that formed because of the war would quickly become a world superpower. Also, other countries got involved, making it as much a world war as a private battle between a colonizing country and its colonized people.

A year into the war, Thomas Jefferson doubted the colonists could hold out much longer. Simply put, the powerful British had more resources than the colonists did. Benjamin Franklin said the colonies could not afford the war. Therefore, Jefferson decided to write a letter to the kings of France and Spain to ask for help.

Jefferson knew his language had to be exact. If France and Spain saw the war as a British civil war, they would not get involved. On the other hand, if Jefferson could convince them that the colonies were their own country, he would convince them that they all shared a common British enemy. He had the support of his fellow colonial leaders. Thomas Paine, Samuel Adams, and John Adams, among others, had already talked publicly about the importance of declaring their independence in order to secure the assistance of France and Spain.

The Second Continental Congress approved the letter on July 4, 1776. (The First Continental Congress of colonial representatives met in 1774 in response to Britain's increased taxes against the colonies. The Second Continental Congress began meeting the following year.) They printed the letter and put it on a ship for Europe.

Within a year, France aligned with America; Spain joined France a year after that. The letter that had convinced them to help the colonies is now known as the Declaration of Independence. Americans celebrate

July 4, the date of the signing of the letter, as the date the colonies declared independence from Britain. However, the colonies' intent was already quite clear to Britain. The Declaration of Independence is, in actuality, the United States' first international-alliance document.

The United States Drafts Its First Constitution

The Articles of Confederation was the United States' first constitution. Colonial leaders started thinking about writing a governing document early in the American Revolution. They needed it to prove themselves to foreign countries so those countries would offer help. They wanted it to encourage a common bond among the colonists. Being in the middle of a war about who would govern the colonies created a sense of urgency about planning what a government after the war would look like.

The Revolutionary War did not end until fall 1781. However, Benjamin Franklin submitted the first draft of the Articles of Confederation to the Continental Congress on July 21, 1775. It took six drafts for Congress to approve the document. Virginia was the first colony to approve it, on December 16, 1777.

All the colonies needed to agree for the Articles of Confederation to be ratified, or officially accepted. By 1779, all the states except Maryland had agreed to the heavily revised document; Maryland signed on in 1781. The Articles of Confederation were ratified on March 1, 1781. They gave states a lot of power and made the federal government very weak. People were scared of a central government. They did not think it could successfully hold such a large, diverse country together.

The colonies agreed to the articles just in time. The war would end later that year, and the colonies would be an independent country. On September 28, 1781, Washington, serving as commander of seventeen thousand French and American troops, began attacking nine thousand British soldiers at Yorktown in Virginia. The Battle of Yorktown raged nonstop until October 17, when Charles Cornwallis surrendered his British troops. That would be the last battle of the Revolutionary War. Peace talks began.

The articles called America "a firm league of friendship." The states would have a lot of power, including approving major decisions, like about war and treaties, but the federal government would have power too. It would run the military, currency, and post office; it would also help states solve their problems.

The federal government was weak in a major way, however: it could not tax the states. It was understandable that, after fighting the British, the states would not want another all-powerful federal government ruling them.

However, without taxes, the central government could not pay for the powers it had or pay its debts from the revolution. Over the years, the Congress tried to amend the articles, so they could tax the states. The idea failed in 1781 and again in 1786. All thirteen states had to agree to the change, and they would not.

Creating a Stronger Ruling Document

The Constitutional Convention of 1787 worked to replace the Articles of Confederation with a better governing document. All the states except for Rhode Island sent delegates to Philadelphia to participate in the convention.

George Washington led the meeting, and the delegates considered James Madison's Virginia Plan first. Critics worried that it gave too much power to larger states, that it looked too much like Britain's Parliament, and that it still did not discuss taxation.

William Patterson's New Jersey Plan gave equal voting power to large and small states. It also gave Congress the power to tax. Alexander Hamilton suggested a duplication of the British Constitution.

In the end, the delegates voted to have a bicameral Congress, or a Congress with two chambers. One chamber would have an equal number of representatives from each

The Constitutional Convention met in Philadelphia in 1787, from May to September, to discuss replacing the Articles of Confederation.

state (the Senate). For the other, states would send a number of representatives based on their population (the House).

Federalists vs. Anti-Federalists

Only thirty-nine of the seventy-four appointed delegates signed the improved document, the Constitution. Some delegates were ill or had some other nonpolitical reason for not signing. Some, called the Anti-Federalists, refused because they felt the Constitution did not do enough to protect states' rights and the rights of individual citizens.

Anti-Federalists wanted a Bill of Rights to secure those more local, individualized rights. They were concerned that a strong federal government, at the expense of states' rights,

Inspiration from the Enemy

The English Bill of Rights inspired the US Bill of Rights. Many of the same ideas, including freedom of speech and owning weapons, are in both. King William III and Queen Mary II signed the English Bill of Rights in 1689. The bill described the rights of citizens and gave the British Parliament more power than the monarchy. The section about rights began:

> *And thereupon the said Lords Spiritual and Temporal and Commons, pursuant to their respective letters and elections, being now assembled in a full and free representative of this nation, taking into their most serious consideration the best means for attaining the ends aforesaid, do in the first place (as their ancestors in like case have usually done) for the vindicating and asserting their ancient rights and liberties declare …*
>
> *That it is the right of the subjects to petition the king, and all commitments and prosecutions for such petitioning are illegal …*
>
> *That the subjects which are Protestants may have arms for their defence suitable to their conditions and as allowed by law …*
>
> *That the freedom of speech and debates or proceedings in Parliament ought not to be impeached or questioned in any court or place out of Parliament …*

William and Mary, co-rulers of England, signed the English Bill of Rights in 1689. It would become an inspiration for the US Bill of Rights.

In this section, the leaders of England promised that citizens would be allowed to petition the king or queen—in other words, to express their needs and ask for support. They said that people could keep guns at home. They also said that their government members could debate freely. Even though the colonists fought to free themselves from England's rule, it made sense they would be influenced by the laws of their original homeland. Plus, individual freedoms just made sense to the colonists!

would lead to dominance by only a few people (likely wealthy ones) and little separation of powers. The Anti-Federalist Party became Thomas Jefferson's Republican Party, or the Democratic-Republican Party, and then later the Democratic Party. Jefferson did sign the Constitution even though it did not align perfectly with his ideas.

For there to be an Anti-Federalist Party, there had to first be a Federalist Party. Led by John Adams, the Federalist Party was the United States' first major, organized political party. Its first goal was to support Alexander Hamilton's Bank of the United States, established in 1791, a bank run and used by the federal government. The Federalist Party's legacy is formidable, even though it lasted until only the 1820s. It succeeded in establishing the national economy and banking systems, the judicial system, and foreign policy and diplomacy principles, much of which exist into the twenty-first century.

John Adams was the country's second president, beginning in 1797, and its one and only Federalist president. (Washington held Federalist values but never officially joined the party, He wished to serve as a nonpartisan president.)

There were topics besides the Constitution that divided the two parties. One of the two parties' biggest disagreements was over relations with Great Britain. The Federalists supported the Treaty of Amity. Jay's Treaty, as it was also known, wanted to establish peace between the United States and Britain. The Anti-Federalists reacted with flyers insisting that the treaty's author, John Jay, should be condemned. Anyone who refused to "put lights in his windows and sit up all night" condemning Jay should also be condemned, they said. Jay's Treaty was signed in 1794.

Governing a New Nation: From Outside Influences to Inside Arguments

The United States did not develop in a vacuum, and it did not maintain its political power without the support of other world powers. Philosophical movements, including the logic of the Enlightenment and the spirituality of the Great Awakening, encouraged the colonists to revolt. The governing documents and rituals of older nations, such as Native tribes and Great Britain, inspired America's founding documents and political processes. International alliances legitimized the young country. All the while, colonies had their own political identities, including their own self-created government styles, and colonists aligned themselves with different early American political parties. The governing of the new nation required exploration, debate, inspiration, and self-definition—it was both an exciting political time and a tense power balance.

The First Flag Maker?

Betsy Ross was born Elizabeth Griscom on January 1, 1752, in Philadelphia. She was the eighth of seventeen children. When she was twenty-one, she married John Ross, and they joined a church George Washington attended when he was in Philadelphia. John Ross would have another connection to America's founding: he was the nephew of George Ross Jr., one of the signers of the Declaration of Independence. Soon, Betsy Ross would have her own role in America's history: Ross family history states that she sewed the first American flag.

Her grandson first told the story to the Historical Society of Pennsylvania in 1870. He said George Ross and George Washington visited his grandmother's upholstery shop in 1776 and asked her to make a prototype flag. She did not like their idea and made several suggestions, including changing the six-pointed stars to more easily constructed five-pointed ones, the ones on the flag today.

This family history has become national lore, but there is no other proof that Betsy Ross sewed the first US flag. There is evidence that she was an upholsterer and that she made flags for the Pennsylvania navy. In 2015, a receipt was found indicating that Washington bought sheets and blankets from the Ross store; this also suggests they met and that Washington may have returned to the store for help with the flag.

Scholars debate whether or not Betsy Ross sewed the first American flag. Nonetheless, she is a celebrated figure in national lore.

There is no proof who sewed the first American flag in the design we recognize today. There is proof that flags were an important sign of political power for the colonists, however. Even before the Revolutionary War began, colonists were flying homemade flags different from the British flag to express their disagreement with British rule. The Grand Union flag, also called the Continental Colors, was the most widely used unofficial flag. It even flew from a US Navy ship, in 1775. On June 14, 1777, Congress passed America's first flag law, resolving that there should be one flag and what it should look like. In February 1778, the French Navy saluted the flag, making it the first acknowledgment by a foreign country of the United States that would come to be.

The debates between Abraham Lincoln (*left*) and Stephen A. Douglas (*right*) during their 1858 run to represent Illinois in the US Senate are a defining moment in American politics.

Chapter Two

A Defining Period: 1800 to 1877

The United States did not escape war during its first full century as an independent nation. In fact, the war that took the most American lives, the Civil War, happened during the 1800s. However, it was also a great century for the US Department of State. Through diplomacy, not just war, the country grew.

The Louisiana Purchase

By the late 1700s, the United States had spread from the East Coast to the Mississippi River. Leaders began considering how they could move settlers into Louisiana, a large stretch of land between the Mississippi and the

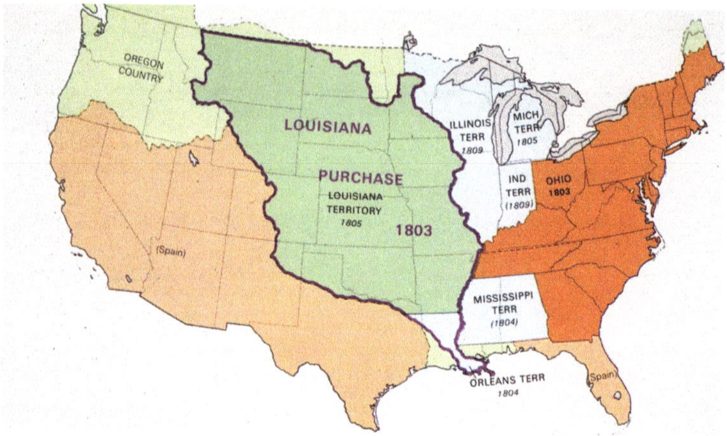

The purchase of the Louisiana Territory in 1803 doubled the size of the United States.

Rocky Mountains. The parcel of land was so big that fifteen of today's states were formed from it.

Spain owned Louisiana from 1762 to 1800. The United States and Spain were already used to negotiating with each other. The Pinckney Treaty of 1795 allowed the United States to use the Mississippi River to transport goods. The United States believed they would have no problem slowly taking over Louisiana.

Then Spain sold the territory to France. Napoleon Bonaparte wanted to use Louisiana to store the sugar produced in the French colonial Caribbean. US President Thomas Jefferson knew he had to be proactive if he wanted the United States to take control of the territory. He sent James Monroe, then governor of Virginia, to help diplomat Robert R. Livingston buy New Orleans and part of Florida from France. He gave them a budget of ten million dollars. By the time they arrived, Napoleon had changed his mind about his Louisiana plans, and he offered to sell a much larger territory for only five million dollars more. In 1803, recognizing the deal, Monroe and Livingston took it without consulting Jefferson.

Jefferson was excited about this sudden expansion, but he was also concerned. Technically, the Constitution did not give the president power to make this large of a purchase. The purchase set a precedent for future presidents and Congresses to assume implied powers. If a choice was considered necessary for the good of the country, the executive and legislative branches could make it even if the Constitution did not explicitly say they could.

The Embargo Act of 1807

As a country, the United States established itself as a political power in several ways. Negotiating with foreign powers to buy land, such as with France to buy Louisiana, was one way. Passing federal laws that exacted American power over another country, such as the Embargo Act of 1807, was another way.

The Embargo Act of 1807 was an act of US economic pressure on Britain and France. The two European countries' battles with each other were negatively affecting the American economy and endangering American sea

★ The Man Behind the Judicial Branch ★

For thirty-four years, from 1801 to 1835, John Marshall led the US Supreme Court with strong opinions. Some of those led to groundbreaking decisions, such as in *Marbury v. Madison* (1803), a court case that established judicial review.

Though he ultimately had a major and lasting effect on the country's judicial process, Marshall was an unlikely candidate to wield such power. Not only had he gone to law school for only six weeks, he had barely attended any school at all. Marshall worked, rather than studied, his way to the top.

John Marshall (1755–1835)

Today, we recognize the Supreme Court as a major part of the judicial branch. In 1801, when Marshall took control of the court, it was considered so unimportant that it was often forgotten. The planners of Washington, DC, even neglected to create a dedicated space for the Supreme Court. The Supreme Court was as unassuming as Marshall, at first—and then, also like him, and because of him, it became a key part of the US government.

merchants. President Thomas Jefferson hoped he could keep his country neutral through policy.

Two incidents directly led to the passing of the Embargo Act. In 1806, France claimed that it could capture any ship, even neutral ships, if they were carrying goods made in Great Britain. That was a direct threat against the United States' ability to trade. Then, in 1807, Britain attacked a US ship, demonstrating that it too felt it had rights over the United States. The USS *Chesapeake* left Norfolk, Virginia, to be stationed in the Mediterranean. Its crew was new, and the ship was filled with a disorganized clutter of supplies. It was not prepared to meet the British HMS *Leopard*. The British admiral told the *Chesapeake* commodore that he wanted to search the American ship for British deserters. When the American refused, the *Leopard* started firing on the unprepared *Chesapeake*. Three Americans were killed, eighteen were wounded, and the ship was all but destroyed.

Because of the embargo, American exports declined by 75 percent, imports by 50 percent. Southern cotton farmers and New England merchants lost their British clients. States talked about seceding, or leaving, the country. Merchants started sneaking goods in and out of the country.

Congress repealed the act in 1809, but that did not solve the problem. Britain and France remained at war, and the United States could not figure out a diplomatic way to stay out of the battle.

The Second Revolutionary War

Britain and France both saw the United States as a possible ally during the Napoleonic Wars. They both attempted to discourage the United States from aligning with their enemy. American leaders were especially uninterested in being coerced by the nation they had recently earned independence from. A group of Republican Congressmen demanded the United States declare war against Britain. The Speaker of the House, Henry Clay, was among them. These Republicans, previously known as Anti-Federalists, were nicknamed the War Hawks.

The War Hawks were mostly from the South. They were interested in the United States growing westward, and they wanted slavery to be allowed in those new territories. However, British-controlled Canada was helping the Native peoples prevent that move. The War Hawks may have primarily wanted to wage war against Britain as an excuse to invade Canada.

President James Madison—and Thomas Jefferson before him—tried diplomacy and applying economic pressures with both Britain and France. The presidents were not interested in fighting, but they were interested in helping their young economy with European trade. Over time, however, Madison sided with the War Hawks. The United States declared war on Britain in June 1812. The war would last thirty-two months, and its largest battle

New Powers for the Judicial Branch

Marbury v. Madison was a Supreme Court case in 1803. It gave the Supreme Court the power to determine if a law is just. Even the legislation made by Congress became subject to judicial review.

Chief Justice John Marshall wrote in the court's opinion:

> *It is emphatically the province and duty of the judicial department to say what the law is … So if a law be in opposition to the constitution; if both the law and the constitution apply to a particular case, so that the court must either decide that case conformably to the law, disregarding the constitution; or conformably to the constitution, disregarding the law; the court must determine which of these conflicting rules governs the case. This is of the very essence of judicial duty …*

A power struggle between the Federalist and the Republican parties led to the court case. Federalist President John Adams wanted William Marbury to be a new judge. When Republican Thomas Jefferson took over the presidency, he refused the appointment. Marbury took his protest to the Supreme Court.

Ultimately, Marshall ruled that Marbury was correct under the law—but that the law was unconstitutional.

happened after the two countries signed a peace treaty, the Treaty of Ghent. The famous Battle of New Orleans in January 1815 was a major US victory. In February 1815, the Senate and the president ratified the peace treaty.

Though Great Britain signed the peace treaty as the losing side, historians agree that the people who really suffered because of the war were the Native peoples. Many Native Americans were killed during the War of 1812; after the war, Great Britain stopped being their allies. The Native peoples were suddenly alone and facing a US government looking to expand into Native lands.

Unstable Political Parties

After the War of 1812, the Federalist Party started to fade. The Democratic-Republican Party, once the Anti-Federalists, appeared to be the only political party in the United States. Yet its members would not stay unified. Under the weight of some major events—including the financial panic of 1819, debate over slavery, and the unusual presidential election of 1824—the Democratic-Republicans started to disagree with each other. They ultimately split into two factions.

Economic Concern

The financial panic of 1819 was major enough that it would have caused issues at any time. For a young country recently emerging from decades of war, it was devastating. Land decreased in value by half in Richmond, Virginia. Land in Pennsylvania that was previously valued at $150 an acre cost $35 an acre in 1819. America experienced its first epidemic of urban poverty. In New York in 1819, 8,000 of the state's 120,000 residents were considered extremely poor. By 1820, 13,000 New Yorkers were out of work or requiring assistance to afford basic necessities. One-third of the nation's population was negatively affected by the financial panic.

The panic was caused by a mix of issues, from loss of jobs as factories closed and loss of wages as cotton prices declined due to government mishandling of credit and land purchases. Its conclusion, in 1823, was just as messy as its beginning. Northerners wished for different solutions than Southerners did, and members of the country's one political party were also divided about what to do.

Social Concern

At the same time as the financial panic, a social panic was happening. Seemingly overnight, slavery became a major topic of debate. Missouri applied to enter the Union as a slave-owning state. If the government let them in, that would mean the Mississippi River no longer formed a border containing slavery to the southeastern states. It would likely set a precedent—it would make it easier for the government to approve slavery in each new western state. At the time, there were twenty-two states in the Union, eleven free and eleven with slaves. Allowing Missouri in as a slave state would tip the balance of the country toward slavery.

The debate about what to do lasted from December 1819 to March 1820. Senator Rufus King of New York led the argument that the federal government had the power to reject a state's slavery preference. Senator William Pinkney of Maryland led the side that said all territories applying for statehood had the same rights that the original thirteen states had—those thirteen joined as free or slave states without any federal interference, and so should all following states. Congress tried to pass more than one bill about the matter, but its members could not agree enough to pass anything.

Finally, Congressmen worked out the Missouri Compromise: Missouri would be allowed in as a slave

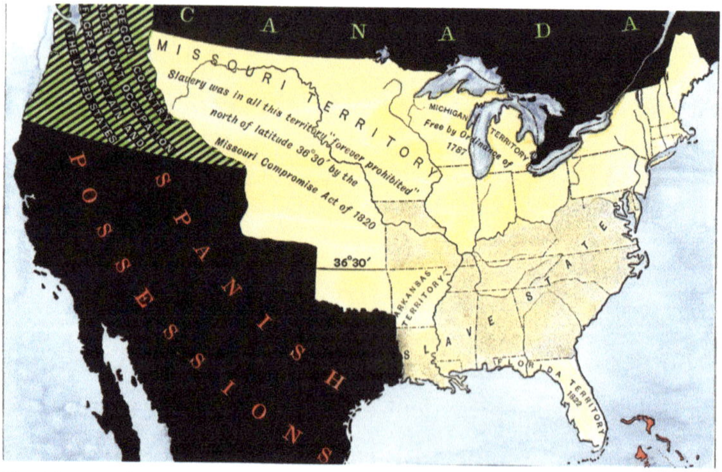

The Missouri Compromise of 1820 said slavery would be prohibited in all American land north of latitude 36°30', except for Missouri.

state; part of Massachusetts would become the free state of Maine. After Missouri, Northern territories joining the Union would not be allowed to have slaves.

Political Concern

The 1824 presidential election divided the Democratic-Republicans further. It began with the closed-door caucus to select the candidate for president. Not everyone in the party agreed that the caucus should be closed to the public. As a result, some did not vote, meaning the candidate chosen did not have the party's full support.

Ultimately, the chosen candidate had a stroke and could not serve. Four candidates stepped forward to fill his space. They were Secretary of State John Quincy Adams, the son of the second president; John C. Calhoun, known mostly in South Carolina; Henry Clay, the Speaker of the House; and General Andrew Jackson, a military hero. Jackson won the people's vote and received the most Electoral College votes, but he did not receive enough electoral votes. According to the Constitution's Twelfth Amendment, the House of Representatives would choose the winner. Clay persuaded them to vote for Adams.

In other words, Adams entered the White House with very little support. He hadn't won the popular vote or the electoral vote. It didn't help that the party had officially split into two: the Jacksonian Democrats and the National Republicans. Adams did not even have a united support system.

Jacksonians believed all white men, regardless of education and class, should be eligible to vote. They believed in manifest destiny, that white Americans were destined to settle the American continent. Jacksonians started off supporting limited powers for the federal government, though as they grew in power, they accepted the idea of the central government also growing in power. They became the modern-day Democratic Party with the next presidential election, in 1828.

The National Republicans, led by Adams and Clay, approached matters differently. They gave merit to educated men over those who had not gone to college. They preferred the idea of focusing on the cities already in the Union to spreading farther west across the continent. They promoted government involvement, including in things like a national railroad system and banking system. They later became the Whig Party and then the modern-day Republican Party, in 1854.

The Civil War: Layers of Politics and Power

Abraham Lincoln became one of the most famous members of the early Republican Party. His political career traced a fascinating time in the country's political history.

The Beginnings of a Political Life

Born in Kentucky in 1809 and living much of his childhood in rural Indiana, Lincoln had only a few months of formal education. He had a natural intellect and also an easy way with people. As a twentysomething working in small-town Illinois, he so impressed his neighbors with the way he ran his general store that they elected him to be their captain in the Black Hawk War of 1832.

The political connections he made while strategizing on the battlefield led to the start of his political career. In 1834, he ran for Illinois state legislature as a member of the Whig Party. Following what the party believed, he voted for government-sponsored infrastructure and protective tariffs. He was against slavery because he viewed it as not being a sound economic decision. While he served in the legislature, Lincoln taught himself law and passed the bar exam, the test to become a lawyer.

As a young man, Abraham Lincoln learned a lot by reading by himself at home.

At the time, a court justice did not preside in one building; each participated in circuit riding, or traveling to different courts in an assigned geographical territory. Even Supreme Court justices did this. Lincoln traveled the circuit too, to pick up cases in several towns rather than just his hometown of Springfield, Illinois.

Making a Name for Himself

Lincoln again ran for office and served in the US House of Representatives from 1847 to 1849. He became the only Whig from Illinois. Following the Whig party line, he spoke loudly against the Mexican-American War (1846–1848). Whigs believed President James Polk was unjustified in fighting Mexico for possession of Texas, New Mexico, and California. Lincoln introduced eight "Spot Resolutions," seeking the truth behind Polk's claim that the United States had a right to the land they were fighting for. The House did not adopt Lincoln's ideas, and his constituents did not like his position on the war, so Lincoln did not run for reelection.

Five years later, political service again called to Lincoln. In 1854, the Kansas-Nebraska Act overturned the Missouri Compromise. Under this new act, settlers of a new state were allowed to decide for themselves if they would allow slavery. A faction of the Democratic Party, the Independent Democrats, and Whig Party members in the North formed the antislavery Republican Party. Lincoln, now morally opposed to slavery, joined the Republicans. *Scott v. Sandford*, an 1857 Supreme Court decision declaring African Americans were not US citizens, was the final push Lincoln needed. (*Scott v. Sandford* is also known as the Dred Scott decision.) Lincoln decided to challenge Senator Stephen Douglas for his seat. Douglas, a member of the Democratic Party, had proposed the Kansas-Nebraska Act.

The Lincoln-Douglas debates of the 1858 campaign became legendary examples of political power struggles. Douglas was a two-term senator seeking a third. This made his campaign a national story. The national news covered the seven debates, held in various cities around Illinois. Some wondered if the country's fate would be determined by those debates. People around the country were on edge because of slavery. The political parties were on edge because of slavery. If a Democratic veteran like Douglas lost, that would demonstrate a serious shift in the nation's politics.

Until 1913, state legislatures elected US senators. On election day in 1858, Illinois voters elected state legislators who in turn reelected Douglas to the US Senate. However, in so many ways, Lincoln won. Douglas's third term was not successful—his party continued to divide. People were so impressed by Lincoln that they asked him to run for president in 1860.

Lincoln's Presidency

Lincoln won the Republican nomination because of his moderate views on slavery, his support of the government paying for infrastructure, and his support of protective tariffs. He went on to win the presidency. All his votes came from the North—Lincoln received zero votes from the slave-holding states. His name was not even on the ballot in ten of the fifteen Southern states.

The omission of his name was not surprising. Before inauguration day in March 1861, seven states had seceded from the country. The next month, the Civil War started. Lincoln had campaigned to lead a country that was already divided.

Lincoln demonstrated unprecedented presidential power. Even before war was declared, he ordered seventy-five thousand men to volunteer for military service. He did not ask Congress before he spent $2 million on the military. He suspended the writ of habeas corpus; he then could imprison anyone arrested on suspicion of siding with the Confederacy for an indefinite period.

Lincoln also made creative use of his right to seize property used in war against the United States. Slaves grew the food and fibers that fed and clothed the Southern Confederate Army. They even served in the Confederacy. At the time, slaves were considered property. In August 1861, Congress passed a confiscation act that officially labeled slaves as contraband. In March 1862, Congress told military officers they were not allowed to return runaway slaves to their masters.

Lincoln delivered his Emancipation Proclamation on January 1, 1863. That speech did not end the war, nor did it emancipate anyone, though it promised freedom. Rather, Lincoln wielded the speech as a rallying tool. The country was fighting for more than itself—it was fighting for human freedom.

The End of a War, a Presidency, and a Life

As the 1864 presidential election approached, Lincoln wondered if he would lose. The country was still at war, and he was often in disagreement with his military officers, his political party, the American people, even his cabinet—he had, after all, surrounded himself with advisers who both agreed with him and disagreed with him. While it was wise to have access to such a complete perspective, that also meant he often had to argue with the people closest to him, an added stress.

Lincoln's worries were baseless. He earned 55 percent of the popular vote, more than he had in 1864. He received 212 of 243 Electoral College votes. In April 1865, soon after Lincoln started his second term and almost exactly four years to the day after the Civil War started, General Robert E. Lee surrendered his Confederate forces to General Ulysses S. Grant. We do not know if Lincoln would have continued to successfully use his political power through Reconstruction. He was assassinated days after the war ended.

This image titled *The First Vote* shows African Americans being allowed to vote for the first time.

Chapter Three

Developing the Home Front: 1877 to 1945

Just as Abraham Lincoln had to deal with the Civil War from the moment he became president of the United States, Andrew Johnson had to deal with the aftermath of the war as soon as he took office. Johnson was Lincoln's vice president during his second term. Johnson became the president after Lincoln was assassinated just a month into that second term and a few days into postwar peace.

Johnson had been a mayor and state legislator in Tennessee and both a member of the House of Representatives and a senator from Tennessee. He was the only Southern senator to stand by the Union, even after Tennessee seceded. Because he was both a Southerner and a supporter of the North, Johnson seemed like a smart choice for vice president.

Presidential and Radical Reconstruction

In May 1865, Johnson announced his Presidential Reconstruction plan. This included amnesty, or forgiveness, for most former Confederates. He left the Southern states alone to reestablish their governments and laws. In response, those states enacted black codes; though slavery had been abolished (Congress passed the Thirteenth Amendment to the Constitution in January 1865), these codes continued to treat African Americans as slaves. Northern Congressmen responded to Johnson's plan by refusing to let representatives and senators from the South into the building.

Andrew Johnson became president of the United States after Abraham Lincoln was assassinated.

The Executive and Legislative Branches Do Battle

In 1866, Johnson vetoed Congress's Freedmen's Bureau Bill and the Civil Rights Bill. The former extended the Freedmen's Bureau, an organization established to help freed slaves in their new lives. The latter said all US-born people were citizens and therefore deserving of rights.

In turn, Congress passed the Fourteenth Amendment, granting citizenship to African Americans. Johnson urged the Southern states not to ratify the amendment.

Congress refused to follow Johnson. The country entered a period known as Radical Reconstruction, and Congress passed the Reconstruction Act of 1867. The act forced all states to vote in favor of the Fourteenth Amendment. It also put the South under federal control and divided the South into five military-controlled zones. The House of Representatives voted to impeach Johnson in 1868. The Senate voted against impeachment—by only one vote.

Ultimately, the Republicans nominated Civil War hero Ulysses S. Grant for president, and he won the 1868 election. Like Johnson, he pardoned the Confederates; unlike Johnson, he supported legislation to help African Americans. The Fifteenth Amendment, ratified in 1870, gave African American men the right to vote. New federal legislation restricted terrorist groups like the Ku Klux Klan (KKK). African Americans even won political positions in the South and the US Congress. Hiram Revels of Mississippi became the first African American US senator

When he became president in 1869, Ulysses S. Grant was just forty-six.

in 1870; that same year, Joseph Rainey of South Carolina became the first African American US representative.

The End of Reconstruction

The Compromise of 1877—which was about the presidential and congressional elections of 1876—ended Reconstruction. Florida, Louisiana, and South Carolina all submitted disputed ballot results to Washington, DC. Congress appointed a commission to determine the winner of each state's electoral votes. This allowed for the possibility of the election to be determined by negotiation, not votes. Moderate Southern Democrats agreed to let Republican Rutherford B. Hayes have the presidency if the Republicans removed the federal troops from the South and let the Democratic Party have control of the Southern states.

The Judicial Branch Gets Involved

The executive and legislative branches (the president and Congress) led the country through Reconstruction. The judicial branch displayed its powers after Reconstruction ended.

The Supreme Court ruled that the Enforcement Act of 1871 (which made Ku Klux Klan meetings illegal), the Civil Rights Act of 1875, and part of the Fourteenth Amendment were unconstitutional.

Because of these rulings, every Southern state redrafted its constitution to make it difficult—or impossible—for African American men to vote. For example, over three years, Louisiana's registered African American voters plummeted from 130,000 to 5,000. Many African American men simply could not meet the requirements of the state's new voting laws.

Louisiana passed a law segregating passenger trains, and the Supreme Court upheld an even broader version of segregation. In the 1896 case of *Plessy v. Ferguson*, the court ruled that public places could be segregated by race as long as they were equal in quality. This was the beginning of the "separate but equal" racism that would not be overturned until *Brown v. Board of Education*, almost sixty years later, in 1954.

Populism Becomes Popular

Even during the Civil War, the US agrarian economy was strong. The United States had lots of land that was good for growing crops, and farmers were wise in their deals selling their crops. However, by the late 1800s, competition from farmers in other countries as well as the rising costs of storing and shipping harvested crops had greatly changed the economic forecast for American farmers. They could only get sixty cents for a bushel of their wheat, where once they had gotten $1.50; a pound of cotton had fallen from $1.25 to six cents. Many farmers had to take out

★ Wyoming and Women's Suffrage ★

When Wyoming became the forty-fourth state, in 1890, it also became the first state to allow women the right to vote. The territory of Wyoming, before it became a state, had allowed women to vote since December 10, 1869. Sixty-nine-year-old Louisa Swain was the first woman to vote in the territory. There were no reports of protests when Swain went to the polling place.

Historians believe there are several reasons why Wyoming granted women's suffrage. One reason was because the people in the territory's government believed in gender equality, at least to a degree. Also, men outnumbered women six to one in Wyoming, and politicians hoped such a law would attract more single women to move to the territory. Drawing people would also allow Wyoming to become populous enough to apply to be a state.

The new law also allowed women to be jurors and hold public office. Esther Morris became Wyoming's first justice of the peace in 1870. These judges preside over minor civil and criminal matters and can perform marriage ceremonies. Morris ruled on forty cases during her career.

mortgages on their land and paid exorbitant interest rates up to 40 percent. Others were forced to become tenant farmers, working land newly owned by someone else and sharing the profit from their crops. In this desperate situation, farmers decided to join together to effect social and political change.

The Grange, the Alliance, and the Party

Oliver H. Kelley, a farmer in Minnesota, organized the National Grange of Patrons of Husbandry Thinking in 1867. Less than a decade later, there were more than eight hundred thousand Grangers, as the members were called, across the Midwest and South. They organized social and educational activities to bring together once-isolated farmers. They also pooled resources to buy storage facilities they could all use.

The Grangers eventually reorganized as the Farmers' Alliance. More than one million farmers, male and female, joined by the 1890s. In the South, the alliance was segregated; the Colored Farmers' National Alliance had more than two hundred fifty thousand members.

The Grangers took the next step and formed an official political party. The People's Party, known also as the Populist Party, argued for policy changes that would help farmers succeed in a manner equal to people working in offices, stores, and factories. These changes included a

Farmers joined together to make the Grangers a powerful political force. Here, Grangers gather for a meeting in Illinois.

graduated income tax; the people, not the state legislatures, electing US Senators; and the government owning the railroads. They also wanted a new federal subtreasury to both store farmers' nonperishable goods and provide fair loans to farmers.

The Populist Party then joined with the Free Silver Movement. Farmers believed that if silver coins were federally approved currency, they could sell their crops for more money. People saw silver as the people's coin, offering economic justice. They were responding to the push by those who were in favor of gold and paper money. Silver mines were growing in number in the West, and people thought that monetizing silver would negatively affect the worth of paper money. Farmers thought more money in the system, including silver, would allow them to raise prices and therefore improve their finances as well as the country's economy.

The Free Silver Movement got the Bland-Allison Act passed in 1878. This made the silver dollar legal. For a while, farm prices improved. When they declined again, in 1887, the farmers demanded the government circulate more silver. Congress agreed with the Sherman Silver Purchase Act in 1890. This law increased the government's monthly silver purchases by half. The act was short-lived, though. Congress repealed it in 1893.

Populism and the Presidency

Social movements, such as the Grangers and Farmers' Alliance, can build their power by becoming political parties, such as the Populist Party. Such a party may start out trying to effect political change among the leaders already holding office. Eventually, however, they may wish to put forward their own candidates for a political seat.

On July 4, 1892, in Omaha, Nebraska, the Populists established their party platform, called the Omaha Platform. They nominated their first presidential candidate. James B. Weaver received more than a million votes in the presidential election, which was impressive for a new party. It also indicated how difficult it would be to break into politics at a high level. The Populist reforms were for everyone, black and white, angering many white Democrats in the South. Others simply did not know much about the young party and did not feel comfortable switching their votes to the party. The Populists did win in some races: they took hundreds of local positions; congressional seats in Kansas, Minnesota, California, and Nebraska; and the governorships of Colorado, Washington, and Montana.

Unrest in All Jobs

Though the Populist Party had a base of farmers, it was open to including other laborers. The party's basic question was "Why do some people get resources and others do not?" American society was starting to feel unfair and divided by class. The Populists were just part of the attempt at a solution to this division.

Worker strikes became common in all industries. People would not come to work until their bosses negotiated with them about their demands for better working conditions or more money. Some of these strikes turned violent. Sometimes they caused so much disruption that federal troops had to intervene.

During the Panic of 1893, there was a national economic depression. In 1894, a businessman named Jacob Coxey organized a march to the Capitol. He wanted to persuade President Grover Cleveland to follow his plan to provide jobs. Coxey's Army, as the press called the impressive group, were stopped at the building's steps. Coxey was arrested for trespassing. Cleveland did not believe government's role was to offer aid to the unemployed.

Another Shot at the Presidency

During the 1896 campaign season, Democrats began to agree with the Populists' pro-silver ideas. Two-term US Representative William Jennings Bryan from Nebraska had fought the repeal of the Sherman Silver Purchase Act. He increased those efforts at the Democratic Convention in 1896. His "Cross of Gold" speech led to the Democrats adopting a pro-silver platform.

Populists were not sure how to respond. If they sided with Bryan, they might lose some of their identity to the more established Democratic Party. If they again nominated a Populist candidate for president, they might split the pro-silver vote, and the Republicans, who supported gold over silver, could win. The Populists eventually supported Bryan, but Republican William McKinley won the presidency anyway. The loss of pro-silver support in the White House also ended up not mattering. A gold rush in Colorado and Alaska, as well as other parts of the world, flooded the market with gold, introducing more currency than silver would have.

The Populists got what they wanted through a different means. The Republicans got the credit, however. The Democrats' base shrunk to mostly poor farmers in the South. The Populist Party disappeared entirely. By the next presidential election, in 1900, farmers' interests were forgotten. Cities became the focus as Republicans found growing support from wealthy businessmen. Because the party held the presidency until the 1912 election, they had time to solidify corporate support.

Political Organizing in Settlement Houses

Political organizing can come from groups of people involved in the same type of work, such as farmers organizing into the Populist Party. It can also come from people facing the same socioeconomic situation. For example, in the late 1800s, people experiencing poverty in the growing American city centers began to organize around their own needs. Settlement houses, places where people could live temporarily and receive social services, provided a physical base.

The settlement house movement was a British invention, but it flourished in the United States. In late 1800s America, when immigration numbers were high and urban poverty was a major issue, settlement houses provided necessary services. They also helped to combat poverty through changes in policy and law.

American Settlement Houses

Stanton Coit founded the first US settlement house in 1886 in New York City. One year later, there were seventy-four settlements in the United States. Three years later, there were over four hundred in the country. Around 40 percent of settlement houses were in Boston, Chicago, and New York; the rest were spread across small cities, most in the Northeast and Midwest. Hull House in Chicago, and others of similar size, helped more than two thousand people each week.

Settlement houses were technically secular organizations, but many groups saw it as their religious duty to help in this way. The Roman Catholic Church, the YWCA, the Women's Home Missionary Society of the Methodist Episcopal Church South, and African American congregations established settlement houses. The latter did so in part because the settlement movement was not free from racial bias. Some white reformers did not think African Americans could be assimilated into society, and they refused to allow African Americans into their settlements. Settlement house allies included civic organizations, women's clubs, business groups, and trade unions.

At a time when women were regularly excluded from business leadership, women led about 50 percent of the major settlement houses. Jane Addams, who ran Hull House, became one of the most well known—she even won the Nobel Peace Prize in 1931.

Addams was born in a small town in Illinois in 1860. She lived an unusual life for most women at the time: she

Immigrants lived and gathered at Chicago's Hull House to share meals and learn new skills.

attended and graduated from college and then traveled in Europe. While in London, she was inspired by the settlement house Toynbee Hall.

Back in Chicago, she leased a large house and named it for its builder, Charles Hull. Hull House offered education to its new immigrant and poor residents—and others in the neighborhood—(such as classes in history, art, and literature and access to an art gallery and libraries) and social services (a daycare center, a kindergarten, a homeless shelter, a kitchen and baths, and staff to help people find work). Within two years, Hull House had expanded its offerings further.

The Political Power of Settlement Houses

Settlement houses and their reformers, like Hull House and Addams, effected political change and encouraged their residents to participate as well. The Immigrants' Protective League and the Juvenile Protective Association, the first American juvenile court, started at Hull House. Reformers lobbied for laws that restricted child labor and enforced schooling for kids. Addams was part of the committee that created the federal bureau that passed the Federal Child Labor Law in 1916. She also campaigned for the founding of the American Civil Liberties Union (ACLU). As President Herbert Hoover's assistant, she spread her help abroad, sending supplies to women and children in countries hardest hit by World War I.

Settlement residents participated in politics too. Hull House provided inspiration—for example, there was a labor museum there, and it provided meeting space for trade unions. The house also provided inspiration because it brought people together in community, and seeing they were not alone in their daily struggles, the settlement house residents felt empowered to advocate for themselves. Residents surveyed their communities and published *Hull-House Maps and Papers* in 1895. This collection of data on housing and jobs encouraged other communities to gather that information about themselves. Armed with this concrete information, the settlements showed the Chicago government that there was real need for amenities and services like neighborhood parks, night classes, and better garbage service. The National Federation of Settlements formed in 1911. Centralizing their efforts in this way helped them to coordinate their political work.

The settlement movement peaked right before World War I. War issues surpassed domestic social issues on leaders' lists of priorities. After the war, as more people became educated and more employment opportunities opened, settlement staff no longer wanted to volunteer. Settlement houses became community centers where people did not live.

Politics and the Environment

People wield political power over not just human systems, such as economies and city planning. Political policies also affect the natural environment in which humans live. The conservation movement was at its height between 1850 and 1920. It provides a unique example of political power. Preserving natural spaces at the federal level is an American creation.

Theodore Roosevelt, who took office in 1901, was known as the conservation president. Conservationists such as John Muir had been concerned about the country's rapid expansion and therefore exploitation of natural resources. Roosevelt was a sympathetic, and powerful, ear. He created the United States Forest Service (USFS) in 1905. Over his terms as president, he protected approximately 230 million acres (93 million hectares).

Named for President Theodore Roosevelt, the Roosevelt Arch welcomes visitors to Yellowstone National Park.

Under President Ulysses S. Grant, Yellowstone National Park became not only the country's first government-protected wild space, created in 1872—it was the first in the world. It was amazing that such a thing happened in a young country interested in private land ownership.

Though Grant signed the Yellowstone National Park Protection Act, the government did not pledge to financially support the park, and there were no laws protecting the wildlife within the park. Park leadership struggled so much against a variety of challenges, including poachers, that in 1886, the US Army took control of Yellowstone. In 1894, Congress passed the National Park Protection Act, or Lacey Act, which gave the army greater power against hunters.

Though the army was good at protecting animals, they were not trained in educating visitors. Stephen Mather, who had made his fortune as a factory owner, began lobbying for a National Park Service. With the backing of other wealthy industrialists and the National Geographic Society, as well as lots of media attention, Mather succeeded. Woodrow Wilson created the National Park Service in 1916.

Though these protected areas prevented land from being privately owned, they promoted the creation of new towns. With the addition of each of the national parks, monuments, battlefields, seashores, recreation areas, and other areas, towns appeared nearby. People could find work with the parks, and railroads increased service because of tourism.

The New Deal

Fights around policies affecting farmers, city dwellers, and the preservation of the environment were all part of what came to be known as the Progressive Movement. Progressivism was the diverse response to America's rapid growth after the Civil War. With new opportunities came the need for new policies. President Franklin D. Roosevelt's New Deal was, in comparison, the political response to lack of opportunity: the Great Depression of the 1930s.

When the US stock market crashed in October 1929, initiating the Great Depression, a lot of people lost a lot of money. People reacted by cutting their spending, and the rest of the world lowered its investment in American industry. In turn, this meant fewer consumer goods were needed, which meant there were fewer jobs, which meant people lost more money—and so the vicious cycle continued. The Great Depression lasted until 1939.

Roosevelt took office in 1933, when the Depression was at its worst. Around fifteen million Americans were

Women's Right to Vote

For almost one hundred years, Americans protested for the right of women to vote. The fight ended with the ratification of the Nineteenth Amendment to the Constitution on August 18, 1920:

> *The right of citizens of the United States to vote shall not be denied or abridged by the United States or by any state on account of sex.*

The Seneca Falls Convention of 1848 brought local suffrage groups together on a national level. Elizabeth Cady Stanton and Lucretia Mott organized the meeting in Stanton's hometown of Seneca Falls, New York. More than three hundred people attended. Most were women, but at least one prominent male leader joined: internationally renowned activist Frederick Douglass.

Unlike the positive response the first female voter in Wyoming received, the convention received a lot of negative press. It took until 1878 for the National Woman Suffrage Association (NWSA) to have enough support to lobby for an amendment. Stanton and Susan B. Anthony founded the NWSA to lobby Congress. It took more organizing, lobbying, a protest at the inauguration of Woodrow Wilson, repeated failed Congressional votes, and even a thrilling tiebreaker in the House of Representatives to pass the amendment.

unemployed. Nearly half of America's banks had failed. As Lincoln and Johnson had before him, because of crisis in the country, Roosevelt had to start his presidency not from a standstill but with a sprint.

The day after his inauguration was the first day of a four-day bank holiday that he ordered. This kept people from taking their money out of the banks; if they had done so, they would have made the banking system worse. At the end of the holiday, Roosevelt's Emergency Banking Act officially reorganized the banks. By the end of that month, his work on that act, alongside Congress, allowed three-quarters of the banks to reopen. The Glass-Steagall Act protected the money of individuals who put their savings in commercial banks. With this legislation, Roosevelt aimed to separate Wall Street from people's other financial interests—if the stock market crashed again, it would not affect people's savings.

Next, Roosevelt led Congress through a series of new policies to increase wages and decrease costs. The country was still in the Prohibition era, when the production of alcohol was illegal; Roosevelt asked Congress to open the country up for beer sales once again. The Tennessee Valley Authority Act of May 1933 provided inexpensive hydroelectric power by damming the Tennessee River. The Agricultural Adjustment Act addressed surpluses of products like wheat, dairy, tobacco, and corn, so that prices would rise. The National Industrial Recovery Act in June permitted unions, to help workers get higher wages; this would be followed a couple of years later by the National Labor Relations Act, which further protected workers' rights.

By April 1935, Roosevelt's Works Progress Administration (WPA) gave people jobs building bridges, creating parks, and producing art. Social Security came into being in August of that year; it guaranteed income to retired people and people unable to work.

Aggressive plans such as the New Deal will always have critics. Roosevelt battled his, and often lost, until the United States entered World War II at the end of 1941. The war industry boosted the national economy, and the Great Depression ended. Even the Supreme Court said some of Roosevelt's programs were unconstitutional. (Roosevelt tried to work around their rulings by "court-packing," adding liberal judges who sided with him.)

Such a bold plan also united previously diverse groups of people. Much of the white working class, many African Americans, and many left-leaning intellectuals all agreed with a lot of the New Deal. People began to approve of a strong federal government that got involved in people's lives. President Lyndon B. Johnson would experiment with a larger federal government with his Great Society, a series of programs akin to the New Deal, during the tumultuous 1960s.

President Lyndon B. Johnson tried to use his political power to solve the high level of poverty in the 1960s.

Chapter Four

Modern Politics: 1945 to Present

Many of the issues the United States contended with in the early 1900s continued to plague the country in the midcentury. In 1960, almost 25 percent of Americans were living below the poverty line. (The poverty line is the minimum level of income needed to afford basic life necessities.) There were great leaps in technology and economic growth, but they were focused in urban centers. People living in places such as the Appalachian region in the southeastern part of the country were suddenly living quite differently than their urban counterparts. People without education, as many were at the time, lost their livelihood when innovation transformed jobs that formerly required little training into careers that required more knowledge. In 1964, almost 25 percent of Americans had not finished high school.

The Great Society

To address the poverty level, President Lyndon B. Johnson introduced the most comprehensive social reform plan in US history, naming his vision "The Great Society." Its policies and programs addressed poverty, inequality, and the environment.

In 1964, the new Office of Economic Opportunity and the Economic Opportunity Act led to jobs and several job training programs for hundreds of thousands of Americans unemployed or underemployed. The Job Corps was similar to the Civilian Conservation Corps of the 1930s. During the Great Depression, President Franklin Roosevelt put hundreds of thousands of unemployed men to work on environmental projects. Johnson's Job Corps also put people to work on conservation projects. A work-study program helped 140,000 Americans afford college. AmeriCorps VISTA, a domestic Peace Corps-type program, began sending volunteers into low-income parts of the United States. Small-business owners and farmers were eligible for new federal grants. Head Start began in 1965, also under the Economic Opportunity Act. It helps children from birth through age five from low-income families prepare for school.

In 1964, almost half of all senior citizens had no health-care coverage. Under the weight of the medical bills for which they had no help, one in three Americans older than sixty-five lived in poverty.

Under Johnson's leadership, Medicare, health coverage for the elderly, and Medicaid, coverage for people with low incomes, became law.

The Elementary and Secondary Education Act passed in 1965. Until this act, only colleges could receive federal funds. After this act, the government could support grade schools and high schools, school libraries, and special education programs. The Higher Education Act provided for the National Teachers Corps, which had the goal of getting qualified teachers in low-income school districts.

Under the Housing and Urban Development Act of 1965, the federal government helped eligible cities with urban renewal and development programs. Businesses and residents had begun moving out of the city centers for the newly invented suburbs. That meant people left in the cities had access to fewer jobs, resources, and housing options. The Department of Housing and Urban Development (HUD) formed. It supported affordable public housing.

The National Endowment for the Humanities (NEH) and the National Endowment for the Arts (NEA) began in 1965. These federal organizations funded museums, public television and radio, and artists and researchers.

Air quality was noticeably bad in US cities in the mid-1900s. The Motor Vehicle Air Pollution Control Act in 1965 standardized vehicle emissions requirements across the country. Before this, politicians had left matters of air pollution to the states. This was problematic. Some states chose to do nothing, and, of course, air did not recognize state borders. Controlling air pollution made sense as a federal policy, and finally, it was.

The Immigration and Naturalization Act of 1965 changed the course of immigration in the United States. Before this act, immigrants had been allowed into the country based on national quotas. Immigrants from countries already well represented in the United States were given priority. That meant Northern Europeans had the greatest chance of being accepted into the country. With this act, preference was given to keeping families together, bringing in people with needed skills, and helping people escape troubled countries, regardless of what country they came from. The Immigration and Naturalization Act could not have come at a more crucial time for people living in Southeast Asia. The region was being torn apart by war. Immigration from Vietnam and Cambodia more than quadrupled. Past immigration policies would not have allowed so many people safe haven in the United States.

The Civil Rights Movement

Part of the reason the Immigration and Naturalization Act of 1965 passed was because of the civil rights movement. Civil rights referred to equal rights for African Americans, but the movement encouraged people to think about positive change for people of all races.

The civil rights movement did not begin overnight, of course. Throughout the years of slavery and Jim Crow laws, there were individual acts of resistance to the racist policies. In the 1940s, Presidents Franklin Roosevelt and Harry Truman both issued executive orders against racial discrimination in the military. These set the stage for the widespread, organized civil rights era of the 1950s and 1960s.

That era is said to have started with a bus ride. On December 1, 1955, Rosa Parks was riding the Montgomery, Alabama, city bus home after work. Buses were segregated by race. When a white passenger could not find an empty seat in the white section, the bus driver asked Parks to give up her seat in the black section. She refused and was arrested.

What followed was a protest unlike any the country had witnessed. For 381 days, African Americans refused to ride the city buses. Because they were the primary users of public transportation, loss of their fares noticeably affected the bus system's budget. Dr. Martin Luther King Jr. led the boycott. Ultimately, the Montgomery Bus Boycott

GATT

After World War II, many countries were eager to rebuild their economies. The war had cost a lot and damaged many industries. World leaders hoped the General Agreement on Tariffs and Trade (GATT), which took effect on January 1, 1948, would help with this.

GATT begins with an explanation of why countries wanted to participate:

> *Recognizing that their relations in the field of trade and economic endeavours should be conducted with a view to raising standards of living, ensuring full employment and a large and steadily growing volume of real income and effective demand, developing the full use of the resources of the world and expanding the production and exchange of goods,*
>
> *Being desirous of contributing to these objectives by entering into reciprocal and mutually advantageous arrangements directed to the substantial reduction of tariffs and other barriers to trade and to the elimination of discriminatory treatment in international commerce …*

In summary, leaders wanted to improve life for all their citizens. They would do so by agreeing to more open trading among countries and the lowering of tariffs, the tax on certain imports and exports.

By the time the World Trade Organization (WTO) replaced GATT in 1995, most trade in the world followed GATT rules; 125 countries were part of the agreement. One effect of GATT on Americans was lower prices on products imported from other countries. Without the trade agreement, tariffs made prices more than 11 percent higher on clothing; sugar cost 8 percent more. Overall, Americans saved $19 billion per year by not having to pay the taxes that would have existed without GATT.

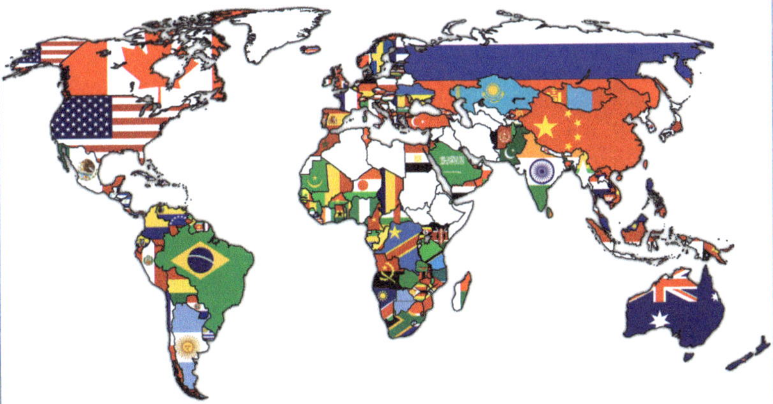

Members of the World Trade Organization (WTO) are noted with their country's flag. The WTO replaced GATT in 1995.

led to the US Supreme Court declaring segregated buses unconstitutional.

The Youngest Activists

Young people played an important role in the movement. As students, they were the ones who integrated schools. Until 1954, many states had laws prohibiting black and white students from going to the same school. On May 17, 1954, the Supreme Court said these "separate but equal" schools based on race were unconstitutional in the court case *Brown v. Board of Education of Topeka*. That did not mean that schools integrated the next day. In fact, communities resisted this decision so strongly that the court had to issue a second ruling, *Brown II*, in 1955. That ruling told the schools they had to start integrating immediately.

Still, it took until the start of the 1957 school year for schools to be ready. A lot of people continued to resist the change. In Arkansas, the governor, a judge, and citizens exercised their political power both for and against integration.

Central High School in Little Rock, Arkansas, had been an all-white school since it opened in 1927. The plan was that on September 4, 1957, it would integrate—black students would be allowed to join the white students there. The local chapter of the National Association for the Advancement of Colored People (NAACP) carefully

Nine high school students bravely integrated Central High School in Little Rock, Arkansas, in 1957.

selected nine African American students to register at Central. Then those nine students attended counseling sessions in the weeks leading up to the first day of school. They had to be prepared for hostility they would face.

Minnijean Brown, Elizabeth Eckford, Ernest Green, Thelma Mothershed, Melba Patillo, Gloria Ray, Terrence Roberts, Jefferson Thomas, and Carlotta Walls would come to be known as the Little Rock Nine.

Two days before the first day of school, Arkansas Governor Orval Faubus said he was going to send the Arkansas National Guard to the school. He claimed this was to protect the Little Rock Nine, but really it was to physically bar them from entering the school.

One day before the first day of school, the Mother's League of Central High School held a protest against integration on the school property. Federal Judge Richard Davies said the school would open to all students, as planned, the next day. The school did indeed open its doors the next day, but the Little Rock Nine were not let in. The state's National Guard prevented them, as did the Mother's League, the Capital Citizens Council, and their angry, racist allies.

Davies began legal proceedings against Faubus, pitting federal judicial powers against state executive powers. President Dwight Eisenhower got involved, telling Faubus to let the students in.

Finally, on September 20, Davies succeeded in having the National Guard removed. On September 23, the Little Rock Nine once again tried to go to school. This time a crowd of one thousand people blocked their entrance. The city police escorted the nine students away.

On September 24, Eisenhower ordered twelve hundred US Army soldiers to Little Rock. Those soldiers successfully escorted the Little Rock Nine to classes on September 25, three weeks after they first attempted to go to school and more than three years after the Supreme Court desegregated schools.

That school year was anything but easy for the Little Rock Nine. They were physically, emotionally, and mentally abused by their fellow students. One of their mothers was fired from her job because she refused to withdraw her daughter from the school.

Faubus was not done exercising his power. After the 1957–1958 school year ended, he closed all of Little Rock's high schools for a full year. During that time, he called for a vote about school desegregation. Little Rock citizens voted 19,470 to 7,561 in favor of segregation. Little Rock's high schools did not reopen until August 1959.

The Rise of Conservativism in the 1970s

In contrast to the 1950s, the 1960s is often remembered as a liberal decade. People protested the Vietnam War and for civil rights and women's rights. A counterculture sprung up, allowing people to participate in activities previously considered taboo or immoral.

However, the decade was also the one in which conservatives became skilled political organizers. At the time, moderate Republicans believed a lot of the same things that mainstream Democrats favored. Far-right conservatives were too extreme to have a chance of appealing to the majority. Conservative Republicans believed their ideals could resonate with a lot of Americans, but they were disorganized and lacking in a clear message.

Then, in 1960, Arizona Senator Barry Goldwater published *The Conscience of a Conservative*, which explained key conservative ideas in clear terms and discounted myths about conservativism. In four years, it went through twenty print runs. Republicans used it as a guidebook to clarify their ideas and communicate them to others.

Conservative Republicans of the 1960s were largely white and in the newly developed middle class. They did not like high taxes, especially because they viewed those taxes as going to poorly managed social programs. During this time of civil disobedience and riots they wanted a return to law and order. They also had lost hope in a strong federal government. The government's actions, or inactions, regarding the Vietnam War and infrastructure negatively affected conservatives' lives.

Goldwater's book was even well received by college students, which is generally considered to be a liberal-leaning demographic. To be a conservative young person at a university in the 1960s was to be part of a counterculture. Conservative leaders wisely began working with college students.

Barry Goldwater was a changemaker in the Republican Party.

William F. Buckley was the conservative founder of the *National Review* magazine. He partnered with conservative fundraiser Marvin Liebman to hold a get-together with one hundred student activists. They formed the organization Young Americans for Freedom (YAF). Just like liberal groups, YAF held rallies and broadcast their message over the radio. Within half a year, it had twenty-one thousand members at more than one hundred college campuses.

In 1961, conservative political activist F. Clifton White traveled the country, coaching conservatives in how to elect delegates to nominate a presidential candidate. Though their candidate, Goldwater, did not win against Democratic candidate Lyndon B. Johnson, the conservatives felt they had won in knowledge and skills gained. Between 1964 and 1968, they positioned themselves as they wanted to be seen, not moderate but not far-right; they focused their platform; they continued to encourage conservatives to effect political change at the local level; and they organized a successful fund-raising drive by mail.

For the 1968 presidential election, Richard Nixon beat out Ronald Reagan, then California's governor, to secure the Republican nomination. Nixon was considered the stable choice over his Democratic opponent, Hubert Humphrey, who had been President Lyndon B. Johnson's vice president. Nixon ultimately won the presidency.

Feminism

Feminism is the belief in equality of the sexes in all realms: social, economic, and political. Like all complex topics, it is difficult to easily define modern feminism. It gets more complicated when we consider intersectional feminism—the overlapping of race, class, gender, sexual orientation, religion, and other identities with sex. It is common to think of feminism as happening in four waves (so far).

The first wave happened in the late 1800s and early 1900s. It was focused on women's suffrage, the right to vote.

The second wave came during the 1960s to 1990s. It began with protests against the Miss America pageant. Feminists rose up against what many people see as a symbol of everyday sexism. In the contest as well as in society at large, women were often treated as objects. To some, they were things to be admired and judged, and they were seen as undeserving of equality with men and unable to be in control over their own lives. With that in mind, second-wave feminists focused on sexuality and reproductive

Estelle Griswold took her fight for birth control all the way to the Supreme Court—and won.

rights. The Supreme Court case *Griswold v. Connecticut* legalized birth control in 1965. *Roe v. Wade* passed in 1973, legalizing abortions. Feminists also sought the passage of an Equal Rights Amendment to the Constitution. Though the first wave happened alongside discussions of slavery and abolition, most feminist groups were homogenous in race, class, and orientation. The second wave diversified—and reflected on how to be more diverse.

The third wave of feminism started in the mid-1990s. The internet has played an important role in shaping this wave. It allows feminists around the world to be more connected. It also allows a degree of anonymity, so gender lines blur.

The fourth wave of the twenty-first century is focused more than ever not just on women's rights but on gender equity. Feminists recognize that racism, classism, ableism, and other concerns are bound together in this fight. Mainstream media and politicians are now more willing to discuss the issues feminists are raising, such as violence against women and women's lack of representation in politics and business.

Environmentalism

Like feminism, environmentalism reemerged as a political issue in the 1960s. Rachel Carson's environmental science book *Silent Spring* was a *New York Times* best seller in 1962. The Clean Air Act of 1963 was the first federal legislation about air pollution control. Dramatic pollution disasters, such as the heavily polluted Cuyahoga River in Ohio catching fire in 1969, made the news. Space exploration also played a role—astronauts sent back photos of Earth, which changed people's perspectives. They were amazed by the planet's beauty and could better grasp how finite its resources are. As the decade changed, major political changes also happened. The president and Congress made four big environmental moves in 1970.

President Richard Nixon delivered a thirty-seven-point speech on the environment to Congress in early 1970. In it, he requested funding, such as $4 billion to improve water treatment facilities; policy changes, such as taxing lead in gasoline and ending dumping pollutants in the Great Lakes; and research, such as figuring out how to reduce motor vehicle pollution and doing a better job of cleaning up oil spills. The Environmental Protection Agency (EPA) started at the end of 1970 to work on Nixon's thirty-seven points and the Clean Air Act's goals.

The amended Clean Air Act (CAA) of 1970 is considered the act that had a real and lasting effect on air pollution in the United States. It launched four key regulatory programs: the National Ambient Air Quality Standards (NAAQS), State Implementation Plans (SIPs), New Source Performance Standards (NSPS), and National Emission Standards for Hazardous Air Pollutants (NESHAPs).

The first Earth Day was also held in 1970. Senator Gaylord Nelson from Wisconsin was influenced by an oil spill in California and inspired by the student anti-Vietnam War movement. He thought that putting such passion behind environmentalism might force the federal government to do more. Nelson asked Republican Representative Pete McCloskey to cochair and Harvard University student Denis Hayes to coordinate. On April 22, 20 million Americans turned out for the first Earth Day.

The first Earth Day, 1970

Twenty years later, in 1990, Earth Day was celebrated around the world, and 200 million people participated. Today, more than one billion people commemorate Earth Day each year, according to the Earth Day Network.

The Religious Right of the 1980s

Though the United States was founded as a country that officially keeps government and religion separate, religion has always played a key role in political decisions and in determining who holds political power. The 1980 presidential election started a political era fueled by the religious right, or the Christian right, meaning people who were both conservative and Christian had the power to effect political change.

Both of the major candidates for president that year, Democratic incumbent Jimmy Carter and Republican challenger Ronald Reagan, said they were born-again Christians. Televangelism, people preaching on TV shows, was important enough to be covered by the news. Televangelist Pat Robertson led a Washington for Jesus rally in 1980 that drew a crowd of 200,000 interested in bringing religion into the federal government. Reagan accepted his party's nomination to run for president with a prayer.

After his landslide election, Reagan continued to invoke God's name publicly. Before Reagan, the phrase "God bless America" appeared once in a major speech by a president; Reagan made the phrase commonplace. It was because of the precedent that he set that political candidates even into the twenty-first century feel they must show some degree of religiosity in order to be successful.

Reagan had a large secular following too, so he did not make the kind of extreme political power moves that members of the religious right hoped for. For example, with regard to the judicial branch of the federal government, he appointed Sandra Day O'Connor to the Supreme Court, and she had a pro-choice voting record. With regard to the legislative branch, he delayed supporting two different pieces of pro-life legislation, the Hatch Amendment to the Constitution and the Human Life Bill.

September 11

Environmental issues provide one modern example of US leaders using political power to make major changes in the world. Reactions to terrorism, another headline-making topic from the late twentieth century on, are another. On September 11, 2001, almost three thousand people were killed in nearly simultaneous terrorist attacks in New York City, Virginia, and Pennsylvania. This unexpected attack within American borders led to an immediate and long-lasting political response. Components of this response include effects on the military, federal departments, and federal laws.

Less than a month after the terrorist attacks, the United States invaded Afghanistan to destroy al-Qaeda, the group responsible. This "war on terror," as President George W. Bush called it, gave the United States license to make other military moves, such as invading Iraq. The United States' involvement in the Middle East has become the longest-running war in the country's history.

Federal departments and agencies were created in response to September 11. Before the attacks there was no Department of Homeland Security, Immigration and

NAFTA

For decades after World War II, the United States was interested in trading at a wide, global level. The country's participation in the General Agreement on Tariffs and Trade (GATT) was one example of that.

Then, in the early 1980s, Canada approached the United States about establishing a trade agreement. The United States liked this idea for two reasons: Canada was already a profitable trading partner, so conducting more trade sounded even better. They also hoped that a US-Canada agreement would be leverage during GATT renegotiations—Europe would know the United States had other trade options and may agree to more US demands.

Soon after the Canada-US Free Trade Agreement was completed in 1988, Mexico asked to join. They did, forming the North American Free Trade Agreement (NAFTA). That reorganization took six years, until 1994. Some Americans were concerned that this agreement would allow companies to move jobs from the United States to Mexico because they could pay workers less there.

Under NAFTA, Canada, Mexico, and the United States cut their import tariffs among them to almost zero, and trade between members grew a lot. It is difficult to know if NAFTA overall hurts or helps each country because of other factors happening in the world.

American soldiers participate in the invasion of Afghanistan in 2001.

Customs Enforcement (ICE) agency, or Transportation Security Administration (TSA).

Since September 11, phone and internet surveillance has increased. In 2013, intelligence-gathering departments had a budget totaling $52.6 billion.

The 2016 Presidential Election

Terrorism was a heated debate topic during the 2016 presidential election. Republican candidate Donald Trump appealed to his voter base by saying President Barack Obama had been weak on terrorism and by linking terrorism to immigration reform. Since September 11, many Americans feared terrorists acting within the country's borders. Trump's belief that terrorists could enter the United States as immigrants resonated with many voters. The ways that the media covered the campaigns of Donald

Trump and Hillary Clinton were also designed to appeal to voter bases.

2016 Campaigns and the Rise of Politicization

In the twenty-first century, the media is considered politicized. Though the news is known for its attempts to be unbiased, it is a human invention and therefore has always been subject to personal prejudices. However, around and after the 2016 presidential election, the media became more divided along political lines than ever before, and people noticed.

Some media outlets are known for their conservative perspectives and others for their liberal perspectives. People often argue that their preferred news source is speaking the objective truth. "Fake news" became a term, indicating stories that were presented as factual but in actuality were unsubstantiated. Often, fake news is circulated to rile up the American public either in favor of a topic or against it. People are now routinely encouraged to do their own fact-checking of news stories to determine the truth for themselves.

Checks and Balances and the Electoral College

Trump's presidential win in 2016 reminded Americans of an interesting facet of the election system the Founding Fathers designed. The Constitution does not say American citizens elect the president. Rather, each state appoints

Donald Trump was sworn in as president of the United States on January 20, 2017.

electors, who choose the president based on how their state votes overall. Each state gets as many electors as it has US Senators and US Representatives. These members form the Electoral College and usually vote for the candidate who received the most votes in their state. Therefore, a candidate can lose the people's vote, as Trump did, but still win the presidency. This also happened in 1824, when Andrew Jackson lost to John Quincy Adams; in 1876, when Samuel Tilden lost to Rutherford B. Hayes; in 1888, when Grover Cleveland lost to Benjamin Harrison; and in 2000 when Al Gore lost to George W. Bush. The Founding Fathers set the election system up like this to prevent a mob of citizens from directing the election. All the power players in America's political system—the executive branch, the legislative branch, the judicial branch, and the citizens themselves—are also part of a checks-and-balances system. They have power and also limits to their power.

CHRONOLOGY

1500s The Mohawk, Seneca, Onondaga, Oneida, and Cayuga agree to the Great Law of Peace. (The Tuscarora later join this group of tribes, known as the Iroquois Confederation.)

1619 The House of Burgesses, the first government with democratically elected officials in the American colonies, begins.

1685–1815
The Enlightenment ushers in an age of reason.

1689 William and Mary sign into law the English Bill of Rights, establishing the rights of English citizens.

1690 John Locke's "Two Treatises of Government," suggesting that the government was created by the people and not by kings chosen by God, is published.

1692 John Locke's "Letters Concerning Toleration" suggests religious freedom and the separation of church and state.

1730s–1740s

The Great Awakening unites colonists through religion.

1776 The colonies send the Declaration of Independence to France and Spain, asking for help in the revolution against Britain.

1781 The Articles of Confederation, the United States' first constitution, is ratified.

1787 The Constitutional Convention meets to fix the Articles of Confederation; they end up writing the US Constitution.

1790s The Federalist Party, in favor of a strong central government and peace with Great Britain, becomes the United States' first political party.

1812 After debate between political parties, the War of 1812 starts.

1830 Caucuses, from the Algonquin word "caw-cawaasough," become the primary way states select candidates.

1890 Wyoming becomes the first state to allow women to vote.

1920 The Nineteenth Amendment to the US Constitution allows women to vote.

1930s President Franklin D. Roosevelt's New Deal programs tries to help Americans survive the Great Depression.

1948 The General Agreement on Tariffs and Trade (GATT) goes into effect, allowing trade without discrimination among countries.

1960s To address the terrible degree of poverty in the United States, President Lyndon B. Johnson introduces the most comprehensive social reform plan in US history, his Great Society plan.

1970 The first Earth Day takes place.

1988 US Congress passes Concurrent Resolution 331, acknowledging Native influence on the formation of the US government.

1994 US President Bill Clinton implements the North American Free Trade Agreement (NAFTA), which President George H. W. Bush negotiated.

2001 The September 11 terrorist attacks lead to the creation of numerous new federal government departments.

2016 The presidential election highlights the influence of the media.

GLOSSARY

burgess A delegate.

caucus A way to choose a political candidate, akin to a primary, but instead of secret ballots, there is a public discussion.

constituents Voters.

deism An Enlightenment idea that God created the world but does not control it.

Democratic-Republicans A political party that began as the Anti-Federalist Party and later became the Democratic Party.

embargo An official ban on trade with another country.

English Bill of Rights This act, signed in 1689, described the rights citizens had, gave the British Parliament more power than the monarchy, and inspired many US documents, including its Bill of Rights.

Federalists A political party defined by the belief in a strong central government.

General Agreement on Tariffs and Trade (GATT) A world trade agreement that lowered tariffs among participating countries; replaced by the World Trade Organization (WTO).

habeas corpus The right to be brought before a judge after being arrested and imprisoned for a crime.

implied powers Powers available to branches of the government that are not explicitly spelled out in the Constitution.

judicial review The US Supreme Court's determination of whether legislation made by Congress is constitutional.

nonpartisan Not siding with a political party.

North American Free Trade Agreement (NAFTA) A controversial trade agreement among Canada, Mexico, and the United States.

ratify Approve.

suffrage The right to vote.

tariff A tax on certain imports and exports.

★ FURTHER INFORMATION ★

Books

Addams, Jane. *Twenty Years at Hull-House with Autobiographical Notes*. New York: The MacMillan Company, 1912.

Gelman, Andrea. *Red State, Blue State, Rich State, Poor State: Why Americans Vote the Way They Do—Expanded Edition*. Princeton, NJ: Princeton University Press, 2009.

Unger, Harlow Giles. *John Marshall: The Chief Justice Who Saved the Nation*. Boston, MA: Da Capo Press, 2016.

Websites

Division of Political History: Exhibitions

http://americanhistory.si.edu/about/departments/political-history/exhibitions

The National Museum of American History hosts virtual exhibitions related to America's political history. View artifacts, read informative texts, and watch web casts of lectures.

U. S. Political Parties

http://www.pewresearch.org/topics/u-s-political-parties

On this website, the Pew Research Center provides studies and articles about American politics, organized by year. Explore up-to-date information about major and minor political parties.

Videos

Hiawatha—1: The Great Law of Peace

https://www.youtube.com/watch?v=79RApCgwZFw

Learn more about the Iroquois Confederacy and the Great Law of Peace, which predate and may have inspired the United States and its Constitution.

Introduction: Crash Course U.S. Government and Politics #1

https://www.pbs.org/video/crash-course-government-1

PBS explains why it's important to study politics and government in this engaging video.

★ BIBLIOGRAPHY ★

Aboukhadijeh, Feross. "Agrarian Revolt." StudyNotes.org, November 17, 2012. https://www.apstudynotes.org/us-history/topics/agrarian-revolt.

Crews, Ed. "The Truth About Betsy Ross." *The Colonial Williamsburg Journal*, Summer 2008. http://www.history.org/foundation/journal/summer08/betsy.cfm.

Dallek, Matthew. "The Conservative 1960s." *The Atlantic*, December 1995. https://www.theatlantic.com/magazine/archive/1995/12/the-conservative-1960s/376506.

Ferreiro, Larrie D. "At Its Core, the Declaration of Independence Was a Plea for Help from Britain's Enemies." *Smithsonian*, June 28, 2017. https://www.smithsonianmag.com/history/its-core-declaration-independence-was-plea-help-britains-enemies-180963857.

"General Agreement on Tariffs and Trade." *Encyclopaedia Britannica*, March 26, 2018. https://www.britannica.com/topic/General-Agreement-on-Tariffs-and-Trade.

Gottlieb, Matthew S. "House of Burgesses." *Encyclopedia Virginia*. Last updated November 10, 2016. https://www.encyclopediavirginia.org/House_of_Burgesses.

"The Great Society." PBS, Retrieved May 1, 2018. http://www.pbs.org/johngardner/chapters/4c.html.

Halloran, Liz "Why Bother with Caucuses?" NPR, February 7, 2012. https://www.npr.org/sections/itsallpolitics/2012/02/07/146513432/why-bother-with-caucuses.

Hingston, Sandy. "11 Things You Might Not Know About Betsy Ross." *Philadelphia*, June 14, 2016. https://www.phillymag.com/news/2016/06/14/first-flag-day-betsy-ross.

History.com. "Articles of Confederation." 2009. https://www.history.com/topics/articles-of-confederation.

———. "U.S. Immigration Since 1965." 2010. https://www.history.com/topics/us-immigration-since-1965.

Horwitz, Tony, and Brian Wolly. "The 10 Things You Didn't Know About the War of 1812." *Smithsonian*, May 21, 2012. https://www.smithsonianmag.com/history/the-10-things-you-didnt-know-about-the-war-of-1812-102320130.

Jacobson, Louis. "Viral Meme Says Constitution 'Owes Its Notion of Democracy to the Iroquois.'" PolitiFact, December 2, 2014. http://www.politifact.com/truth-o-meter/statements/2014/dec/02/facebook-posts/viral-meme-says-constitution-owes-its-notion-democ.

Klein, Christopher. "The State Where Women Voted Long Before the 19th Amendment." History.com, August 26, 2015. https://www.history.com/news/the-state-where-women-voted-long-before-the-19th-amendment.

Leach, Llewelyn Susan. "GATT Is Good for the Economy—And for the Average American." *Christian Science Monitor*, 1993. https://www.csmonitor.com/1993/1210/10083.html.

Marquand, Robert. "Colonial Sermons Laid Groundwork for the Revolution." *Christian Science Monitor*, July 3, 1987. https://www.csmonitor.com/1987/0703/askip.html.

McNamara, Robert. "The Full Story of Thomas Jefferson's Embargo Act of 1807." ThoughtCo., April 10, 2018. https://www.thoughtco.com/embargo-act-of-1807-1773316.

Native American Caucus of the California Democratic Party. "Tribal Sovereignty: History and the Law." Retrieved May 1, 2018. http://www.nativeamericancaucus.org/content/tribal-sovereignty-history-and-law.

Nordell, Jessica. "Millions of Women Voted This Election. They Have the Iroquois to Thank." *Washington Post*, November 24, 2016. https://www.washingtonpost.com/posteverything/wp/2016/11/24/millions-of-women-voted-for-hillary-clinton-they-have-the-iroquois-to-thank/?utm_term=.a9bac473ba91.

NPR. "The Supreme Court's Failure to Protect Blacks' Rights." *Fresh Air*, February 24, 2011. https://www.npr.org/2011/02/24/133960082/the-supreme-courts-failure-to-protect-civil-rights.

Paul, Catherine A. "Jane Addams (1860–1935)." VCU Libraries Social Welfare History Project, Retrieved May 1, 2018. https://socialwelfare.library.vcu.edu/settlement-houses/addams-jane.

Rampton, Martha. "Four Waves of Feminism." Pacific University. Last updated October 25, 2015. https://www.pacificu.edu/about/media/four-waves-feminism.

Siegel, Robert, and Art Silverman. "During World War I, U.S. Government Propaganda Erased German Culture." NPR, April 7, 2017. https://www.npr.org/2017/04/07/523044253/during-world-war-i-u-s-government-propaganda-erased-german-culture.

"U.S. National Parks—In the Beginning." *National Geographic*, May 26, 2010. https://www.

nationalgeographic.com/travel/national-parks/early-history.

Wade, Louise Carroll. "Settlement Houses." *Encyclopedia of Chicago*. Retrieved May 1, 2018. http://www.encyclopedia.chicagohistory.org/pages/1135.html.

World Trade Organization. *The Text on the General Agreement on Tariffs and Trade*. Geneva, Switzerland: World Trade Organization, 1986. https://www.wto.org/english/docs_e/legal_e/gatt47.pdf.

INDEX

Page numbers in **boldface** are illustrations.

★ ABOUT THE AUTHOR ★

Kristin Thiel lives in Portland, Oregon. She has written many books for Cavendish Square Publishing, on topics ranging from science and technology to history and current affairs. Her first book was a biography of Dorothy Hodgkin, a Nobel Prize–winning crystallographer. She is also the author of *Discovering America: American and National Identity.*